TO: Dawn King

From: Debbie Bragg

11-9-01

Blessings From Above

PAINTINGS BY

*Debbie
Kingston
Baker*

HARVEST HOUSE PUBLISHERS
EUGENE, OREGON 97402

Blessings from Above

Copyright © 1998 Harvest House Publishers
Eugene, Oregon 97402

ISBN 1-56507-813-6

Artwork designs are reproduced under license from © Arts Uniq'®, Inc., Cookeville, TN and may not be reproduced without permission. For information regarding art prints featured in this book, please contact:

Arts Uniq'
P.O. Box 3085
Cookeville TN 38502
800-223-5020

Design and production by Garborg Design Works, Minneapolis, Minnesota

Harvest House Publishers has made every effort to trace the ownership of all poems and quotes. In the event of a question arising from the use of any poem or quote, we regret any error made and will be pleased to make the necessary correction in future editions of this book.

Manufactured in China.

98 99 00 01 02 03 04 05 06 07 / IM / 10 9 8 7 6 5 4 3 2 1

Reflect upon your
present blessings, of
which every man
has many…

CHARLES DICKENS

For family and friends,
the rose and dove,
a child's smile,
a life of love…

How blessed we are!

May our hearts be
ever-thankful for the
tender blessings
from above.

4

May there always be work for your hands to do

May your purse always hold a coin or two

May the sun always shine upon your window pane

May a rainbow be certain to follow each rain

May the hand of a friend always be near to you and

May God fill your heart with gladness to cheer you.

AN IRISH BLESSING

5

Blessed are they who have the gift of making

friends, for it is one of God's best gifts. It

involves many things, but above all, the power

of going out of one's self and appreciating

whatever is noble and loving in another.

THOMAS HUGHES

6

©Debbie Kingston Baker

I Thessalonians 5:17

I will lift up my eyes unto the hills

from whence shall come my help?

My help comes from the Lord

Who made heaven and earth.

THE BOOK OF PSALMS

9

Blessed are the poor in spirit,
    for theirs is the kingdom of heaven.
Blessed are those who mourn,
        for they shall be comforted.
    Blessed are the meek,
        for they will inherit the earth.
Blessed are those who hunger and thirst for righteousness,
            for they will be filled.
        Blessed are the merciful,
            for they will be shown mercy.
        Blessed are the pure in heart,
                for they will see God.
        Blessed are the peacemakers,
            for they will be called the sons of God.

THE BOOK OF MATTHEW

Let us observe this day with reverence and with prayer that will rekindle in us the will and show us the way not only to preserve our blessings, but also to extend them to the four corners of the earth.

JOHN F. KENNEDY

Thanksgiving Proclamation, 1961

13

whatever is true, whatever is honorable, whatever is right, whatever is pure, whatever is lovely... if there is~

© Sally Kingston Baker

- any excellence and if anything worthy of praise, let your mind dwell on these things.

14

May the Lord, the God of

your fathers, increase you a

thousand times and bless

you as he has promised!

THE BOOK OF DEUTERONOMY

We make a living by what we get,

but we make a life by what we give.

WINSTON CHURCHILL

It is more blessed to give than to receive.

THE BOOK OF ACTS

Lord, behold our family here assembled.
We thank you for this place in which we dwell,
for the love that unites us,
for the peace accorded us this day,
for the hope with which we expect the morrow;
for the health, the work, the food and the bright skies
that make our lives delightful;
for our friends in all parts of the earth. Amen.

ROBERT LOUIS STEVENSON

19

By wisdom a house is built; And by understand

the rooms are filled with all preci

20

's established; And by knowledge

Debbie Kingston

d pleasant riches.

Proverbs 24:3,4

He who extends mercy offers

an immeasurable gift from the

very heart of God.

E.B.S.

Hush, my dear, lie still and slumber.

Holy angels guard thy bed.

Heavenly blessings without number

Gently falling on thy head.

ISAAC WATTS
A Cradle Hymn

25

To everything there is a season, and a time for every purpose under heaven:

a time to be born, and a time to die; a time to plant, and a time to pluck up

that which is planted; a time to break down, and a time to build up; a time

to weep, and a time to laugh; a time to mourn and a time to dance; a time to

embrace, and a time to refrain from embracing; a time to seek, and a time to

lose; a time to keep, and a time to throw away; a time to tear, and a time to

sew; a time to keep silence, and a time to speak; a time to love, and a time to

hate; a time for war and a time for peace.

THE BOOK OF ECCLESIASTES

27

Dear Father, hear and bless

Thy beasts and singing birds;

And guard with tenderness

Small things that have no words.

AUTHOR UNKNOWN

28

Blessed are the gentle, for they shall inherit the earth.

Matthew 5:5

29

The Lord will guard your going out and your coming in from this time forth and forever.

Psalm 121:8

© Debbie Kingston Baker

30

The Lord bless you, and keep you;

The Lord make His face shine on you,

And be gracious to you;

The Lord lift up His countenance on you,

And give you peace.

THE BOOK OF NUMBERS

An Irish Blessing

May the road rise to meet you.
May the wind be always at your back. May
the sun shine warm upon your face,
the rain fall softly on your fields.

And until we meet again
may God hold you
in
the hollow of His Hand.

Debbie Kingston Faby ©